To Tub.

Writing a poem is like
making love to a beautiful
woman

Best wishes.
Brian.

Waiting for Ben

and other poems

BRIAN D HADDOCK

authorHOUSE®

AuthorHouse™ UK
1663 Liberty Drive
Bloomington, IN 47403 USA
www.authorhouse.co.uk
Phone: UK TFN: 0800 0148641 (Toll Free inside the UK)
        UK Local: (02) 0369 56322 (+44 20 3695 6322 from outside the UK)

Published by AuthorHouse 12/13/2022

ISBN: 978-1-7283-7952-4 (sc)
ISBN: 978-1-7283-7951-7 (e)

Print information available on the last page.

Any people depicted in stock imagery provided by Getty Images are models,
and such images are being used for illustrative purposes only.
Certain stock imagery © Getty Images.

This book is printed on acid-free paper.

To Katie for putting up with me

2002

Hesiod's Entropy, a Violent Birth!

Plates grinding entropically onward,
Chasms expose entropic interiors,
Engines expire, surface cools,
Hesiod's Titans no longer battle
Anger dissipates, layers of hate cool and crack,
Entropy Echoes,
Reverberating along the convoluted paths of subatomic particles,
Incarcerated within the hermetically sealed
Within the collider tube

2002

On the circularity of Water

Transporting millennia in entropic cycles,
Double Decker's on ring road,
Junctions are entropic doorways
Hermetic seals are undone when one bifurcates.

Entropic Hinges

Valves are entropic hinges
The more complex a system is, the more energy is needed
to navigate it.
Coupled with the more components needed,
is the requirement for more service to maintain.
Complexity is entropy,
Complexity accelerates entropy.

2015

A gloss

Gleaming cherry, glossy
A gloss,
Given gloss by light,
Light by circumstance,
thrown onto the cherry.

Perfect, uncompromising,
apex of all senses,
or
devoid of any sense,
Beyond sense,
The curves, surface tensions, every pore.

2015

October Morning

October morning.
Splitting the photon with the degree of a sphere.
Shadows of David's leg,
falling across the grass,
marking the fence,
faint warmth marks the inevitable cycle.

2015

Tiger

Tiger clad,
Witch like limbs,
turned inside out,
languid, prowling siren

2015

Buckled Vortex

Buckled Vortex,
Cold polar weight sinking,
decoupled, unhinged,
free falling.
A magnetic, mechanic draw
puncturing the skin,
solid oozing flow.
Slabs of winter mornings bearing down on the surface of
the Earth.

Hangover

Accelerated doppler effect of crushing feet and screaming
kids,
bass thundering,
working out a hangover rhythm,
tired body.
Pain full, resonating internal fracturing.
Hiding my own entropy that has suddenly made itself
present.

Oct 2016

Norfolk

Bloated, billowing pillows,
scattered, tumbled collection,
delimitating the line of space from right here to 'out there'.
Angled slate of foreground,
where the middle distance has dropped off an old still edge –
angled field.
Pinpointed, illuminated with a scratch of Naples.

May 2019

Ribblehead

Stop,
start.
Dropping down,
step by step.
Wet,
cold – the thought of the warm wind coming off the underground.
Menacing,
looming light,
on the right.
A howling,
slow,
methodical mist
drifting across the barren,
soulless plain.
Emanating from the vents that span two lumps,
the gas moves slowly in bands.
A menacing gas.
A low bass sound, inaudible to the human ear
but deathly penetrating,
landing on everything,
contaminating souls,
fallen sheep
and
black pools.
Exhausted.

April 2022

Scrape

The muppets,
plonking, bobbing,
up and down,
in and out.
Scrape, scrape, scrape

Each new scar,
carved into the powdery realm,
marks another act.
Measure,
Cartesian lines between zero and one.

April 2022

Newton's Stupidity

A pull here,
correct.
A shove there,
correct.
Mind and body in harmonic syncopation.
Adrenalin – control – adrenalin – control,
error,
miscalculation,
a slip,
retrieved – retrieved – back to control.
Speed up,
slow down,
speed up, slow down.

April 2022

Quantum Ski Slope

'What's happening above?'
'When?'
'Before now'
'Where?'
'Prior to where we are',
'now?'

April 2022

Hegelian Ski School

'Where to start?'
'Take the path we made yesterday'
'We made? Not made by history?'
'Carved out of history'.
'In what time frame?'
I's the path not totally exposed to the meaningless contingency of natural necessity?'
'Where does it lead?' When do we arrive?'
'No arrival, just ever repeating.'

July 2022

Quads of Steel

She was set like a climbing frame,
quads of steel,
She could bury you, marry you, flog you.
Her softer parts were remote,
an Atoll.
She stood alone.
Cold silent column.

Drum tight lycra stretched over her anvil pubic bone.

July 2022

Salad bowls

Salad bowls, strange attractors,
dust in carpet underlay,
accumulated human fractals,
heaped in corners of entropy,
forgotten conversations stacked in the dark.
The pendulum still moves,
to the decay of a tooth and a Nation.

Dan's Rage

Atom bombs,
Intestines.
The sun raiding his temples,
a hundred tons of compressed gas in his lungs.
He is vibrating with sickness,
hate consuming every molecule within him.
A swarm of stings,
debilitating arrows of poison,
a combustible paralysis
a cellar of furnaces,
high pitched napalm
searing through his rollercoaster of
corridors
capillaries
and
cartilage.
Microscopic hit squads.
Fibre optic snipers infiltrate the ante chamber,
ripping the connections apart,
the wires,
the sockets,
the fuses.
Cyber anarchism from within,
whilst the medieval crushing force of millennia snap his
frame with Pagan doors
and carefully placed rocks.
They end him.

Expired, gone.
A new present has sculpted a new future, a new past.
The incandescence temporarily paused,
soothing glacial song
dances and smothers the Caldera.
The atomic bombs rest their weary heads,
for now.

Aug 22

Dent Night

I walked through centuries,
under a metallic sheet of night sky.
The street sculpted by a billion tired souls.
Needles of light from distant suns
resonated and filled the
bowl of black
with harmonic synchronicity,
saturating singularity,
present on present.

Aug 22

Cows with Crossbows

Cows with Crossbows.
Sheep with hands
play Furr deli

One Hundred and Sixty Thousand

To steal bread from hungry mouths
and
to turn on one another.
To dull their wits with gibberish
and
cannot use their ears and eyes.
Oil drums of poison fermenting under the canvas.

Aug 22

Neon

Neon
Orange Plastic Chairs
White Bags of Flesh
Orphans of the Underground,
displaced souls
Ceausescu's forgotten Children.

Aug 22

Double Denim

Double Denim.
Two stroke dreamer.
Pot bellied
and as
tired as a dream that wants to die

Ceramic insulator pots,
glitter in the early morning sun,
intersecting lines across a deep field sky,
stringed instruments of the wind.

Aug 22

All the Twisted Meadows

All the twisted Meadows
All the Cathedrals standing in the sunlit gunfire
All the Children scarred by Hope
All the drawings never drawn
All the Ropes filled with fury
All the Sinks stained with horror
All the bike wheels framed by midnight
All the tired pages of songs
All the empty Go-Carts
All the death accumulated in telephone wires
All the ashes of arguments
All the blood-soaked granite
All the contradictions heaped in teaspoons
All the clutter of anonymity
All the nights of coffins
and
Bags of Sugar
All the poisoned Ravens,
suffocated by Rhymes
All the Supernovas,
Silent sacrifices
and
Robot Arms
All the kettles and dried riverbeds
All the gun shots and embroidered silk
All the car crashes and perfume
All the stagnant pools and Rainbows

All the Tiles and squandered thoughts,
promises
and
excuses
All the Taps left running and Crystal Devices
All the Arsonists and Alpha Centauri
All the Transistors and Archways
All the bleached beaches
and
incarcerated food markets
All the Stone Age children
and
Petrol Stations
All the empty cartons of mountains
All the Methane
and
Church Choirs
All the pressing engagements
and
Cancer Patients
All the windswept ideals
and
tides of wires and rivets
All the broken windows
and
meat hooks
All the train carriages
and
cemeteries
All the Liposuction
All the Pedantry
and
closed coal mines

All the disabled wheelchairs
and
kitchen surfaces
All the Netflix movies
and
old people's homes
All the Theatre props
and
Holidays in Devon
All the retired Porn Actors
and
Radio Controlled Cars
All the listed buildings
and
Looted memories
All the surgical instruments
and
Caricatures
All the Manhole covers
and
Games of Scrabble
All the mathematical equations
and
Brain Tumours

Aug 22

I have tasted Eclipses

I have tasted Eclipses,
and swallowed dusk.
After death comes nothing hoped for nor imagined.

Aug 22

Dialectics & Heraclitus

Thesis
Anti-thesis
Synthesis
From the strain of binding opposites comes harmony
When is elastic at rest?
What is scattered,
gathers,
What was gathered
blows apart.

Aug 22

Proximity of War

There is a war in the Ukraine,
but it is not the same.
the refugees,
look like you and me,
white faces,
ski jackets
and
Nike's.
The Proximity of War
reveals the cowards and the heroes.

Aug 22

The Big Bang

The Big Bang,
bathtub of bubbles,
multiverse

'Do you want to be a Scientist?'
'He's really a Poet'
'The first Scientific Poet!'
'No!'
Poetry is Philosophy.
Philosophy is Theory.
Good Science is simply to disprove Theory.......
Plato
Socrates
Pythagoras
Empedocles
Democritus
Heraclitus
Parmenides
Epicurus
Anaximander
Xenophanes
Diogenes
Zeno of Elea
Anaximenes of Miletus

Aug 22

Tick Tock, Tick Tock

Time is made to be wasted
Time is only imagined
Time is relative
Time is measured

Tick Tock, Tick Tock

Space Time
Play Time
Day Time
Night-time

Geological Time
Cosmological Time

Aug 22

Scattered Ashes

Scattered ashes,
Three-legged Grey Hound
Empty rooms, empty chairs
The crushing weight of loneliness
'I talk to my Dog'
It has the saddest face I've ever seen.
Fourteen years of fear

Aug 22

Tectonic Visions

Hungry streams
Fractured moments of children laughing
The inescapable sun
Tectonic visions,
glacial harmonics
The trickle of water
filling each hour.

Aug 22

Veneer by the Sea

I feel nothing today,
anesthetised by the sun.
No images, no contradictions, no depth
veneer,
surface,
metallic Jelly Fish,
bleached plane.
Diebenkorn horizon divided by breakwaters,
transections of wood and water.

Aug 22

Nuclear Forces

A sticky universe
of anthropic contradictions,
porous solitude,
crossing
infinite transections of Diamond Light.
Huge milky areas of silence,
suspended from the scaffolding of nuclear forces

Interrogated by the neutron,
violated by the proton,
scrutinised by the electron.
Dirty particle f!
Eating away at my existence,
turning my days full of sunlight
into
a multi storey car park of heroin addicts.
Crematoriums for the unlived.

Aug 22

Shimmering fabric energy

Shimmering fabric energy
diffuse light,
decoupled histories,
shards of life, dissembled,
basking in the afterglow of the Big Bang.

Aug 22

Boundaries

Boundaries,
exotic opposing forces.
A temporal network of related existence
Spinning disk of erotica,
blades of arousal.
Skin on Skin

Aug 22

Pumping Dirty Loads

Gas masks,
Grease Pumps
Excrement and Concrete,
Brake dust,
Tears,
Scar tissue
Alternating current
Catenary hanging in the dusk from tired stretched out limbs
fed by
Cantilevered monoliths.
Towers impregnated by sub stations,
Pumping dirty load after dirty load.

Aug 22

Heat Stress

Beech, Birch and Sycamore
fill the hospital wards.
Stressed,
Anxious,
Panicked.
Arrested transpiration,
derailed symbiosis.
Outside the exhausted landscape has been
carved up into a geometric Hell
Mechanically raped.
Monoculture fans the flame of greed.
Tarmac for the Rabbits.
Asphalt for the Crows.

Aug 22

Drainpipe

In spasmodic episodes
a drainpipe
vomits mouths of accumulated dead vegetative matter
onto the silent angry pavement.
The horrors of the city air,
molecularly bound
rejected back at our feet.

Aug 22

Summer Downpour

The warm afternoon sky empties its pockets over London.
Towers of convection,
leap from pavements,
draw themselves high on ladders of toxins,
cooling as they climb.
Attrition in ascent.
Decelerating as their heat is wasted.
Surface tension,
animated suspension,
bubble against bubble.
A sigh as gravity reclaims its prowess.
The loose change falls,
bounces off the slabs of concrete and asphalt below,
chaotically tumbles down drainpipes,
Ricocheting off pavements and bounces off glass.

Aug 22

Flash of Violence

Flash of violence,
like sunlight on a sword,
twisted anger
and
hilarity.
Mutilated futures
destined from a disruptive present

Aug 22

Heartbeat in Spain

I hear my own heartbeat,
heavy, tired
plodding through my ear
onto the pillow.
Feeling slightly nauseous.
Lifeless puddle of flesh and organs,
transparent,
embedded in the void
bound in nothingness,
absent in the current.
I hear the faint plodding of percussion
from a distant exhausted party

Aug 22

Bukowski

She was like a machine gun tower
from World War One.
He was like a piece of silk
tacked to a door frame
that lead nowhere.
Only Bukowski could marry them.

Aug 22

Terraced Houses

Terraced houses,
broken walls.
Motorbike parts
wheelie bins full,
with wasted days and wasted nights.
Drab net curtains
collect useless conversations,
promises and ideas
never executed.
A curtain of dog's p
on the ankle of a lamp post
maps a delta on the pavement.
An orange line tumbles over the curb stone.

Aug 22

Bagged Mouse

Bagged Mouse,
broken glass
Chimpanzee ready to box
with spherical fists.
Frame.
Symmetry.
Pool lights and Ursa Minor.
Voyeur Dragon Flies.
Glorious breasts.

Aug 22

Nebulous Ideas

Nebulous ides and images
float through my mind,
bounce and jostle one another.
Intersections of wires
stretch and hang,
black and white,
in and out of existence,
frame after frame.
House Martins carve up the hot thick soupy sky.

Aug 22

Grey Ash

The Grey Ash
of a billion emptied ash trays
singeing the souls of my feet.
Percussion,
spread across centuries.
The mountains are silent.

Aug 22

Chaos Prevails

First there was light,
artificial.
Framed by trauma,
Euclid's fiction,
dismembered.
Chaos prevails
as the geometry of innocence is unwoven.

Aug 22

Spain Night

The crumpled fabric
of a billion,
glittering Suns
stretched out before me.

Aug 22

Snip, snip, snip

Snip, snip, snip.
Mandibles,
weapons.
A belly fully of toxins.
An undercarriage of war machinery.
Reconnaissance after reconnaissance,
raid after raid.
A landscape of dismantled breakfasts,
a sprawling city of sugar and acid,
terrorised by the black and yellow armies.
Cities of action.
A cartoon of evolution.

Aug 22

Dead Rat

Poor thing,
must have been there for weeks.
Its spilled guts
welded to the ceramic floor,
mummified,
empty.
Its dried carcass
exhausted.
4th and 3rd dimensions extinguished.
Eaten from within
by a million microbes,
a hungry parasitical army
that have now been dispatched to a fresh expunged soul.

Midnight Gravity

Pools of midnight gravity
welds me
to a subterranean dream.
Suppressed
under the Galactic weight
of a billion Suns.
Pins my core to a to a brutal,
silent song.
Entombed,
buried,
under tectonic layers of inky felt
as the tired trains crawl.

Aug 22

The Lightning Storm

Black tons of night,
shattered
in Blue Bottle Time
by Atomic light.
My Hiroshima shadow cast to the wall.
Nights with Trinitite edges.

Aug 22

The Long Road to War

February 1890
Germany
'We don't want to put anyone in the shadow,
but we do want our place in the Sun.'
August 1945
Japan
Two places in the new Suns
Germany
in the shadows.

Aug 22

 awoke

I awoke,
to the sound of a train in the distance,
slipping West.
Jewels of the Sea,
splinter,
As the waves unfold over the Sea Wall.

Aug 22

Keats

Keats aesthetic delusion.
Keats,
dissociated,
fractured
recollection of England,
that never was.

Aug 22

Scoffing

All the fat people
Scoffing their breakfasts.
Scoffing,
scoffing,
scoffing.
Flabby Pelican necks,
flapping around in furious mastication.
A city of cellulose.
Death lurks in the shadows of the canteen.
Insulin seeps through the walls

Aug 22

The Model Village – Order & Entropy

Amplified entropy.
The model village.
Well clipped,
well maintained.
Hedgerows of death
At the edge of entropy.
Painted lines,
geometric butchery,
channels of misplaced logic
over Art.

Aug 22

Thermic Welds

Thermic welds,
fishplate holes,
Pandrol clips
and
slide chairs.
The UP train
rumbles through as the entire formation
sighs a relief
with the passing of each bogie.

Aug 22

Under Bridge

Ghosts of ancient machines,
Traverse the iron road,
Under bridge
And released into the glory of the West.
Sea spray and granite,
A symphony of metal on metal.

Daniel got rolled

Bobbing,
undulating,
washing in and out with the foam.
Dance around the jaws of the Sea,
Where the break meets the step.
Daniel got bitten,
rolled,
and driven.
Crushed and trampled
by the weight of atmospheres.
Dragged across the millennia of broken stone.
Skin retarded by shingle.
Blood drawn in an instance
across the expansive slabs of time.
Human internal flow wedded to the slow tectonic waltz.

Sep 22

Coleridge

As I sit
idle as a painted ship
upon a painted ocean.
From a torn sky
a shaft of light
punctures the heavy, tired sky,
illuminating Exmouth.

Sep 22

Doug & the Sea

His strength diminished,
given up,
to the Sea.
The moon
carves out time with every wave.

Sep 22

Coleridge fire

The death fires
danced at night
upon the cracked
edges of the day.

Sep 22

Mysticism

Is the germ of mysticism
not extinguished
by the alien shine of un-concerning stars?

Sep 22

Pander

Suffocate the children
with fear and paranoia.
Crush their enthusiasm,
their wonder
with hidden shadows and cynicism
in the rotting bowels of
murderers and paedophiles.
While others nurse the infant diamond in the mine.

Sep 22

A grey Sea

Iridescent.
Elastic surface.
Stretching
and contracting.
Shimmering power
under a weightless sky.

Sep 22

13 Years

Actions parked
on 'Post it' notes.
Synthetic oil,
electric guitars.
First day of term
and
the hum of the North Circular Road.
Time hangs from the
doorknob.

Sep 22

Warm Tube Ride

Subterranean intersection
of
fallopian tunnels.
A vacuum,
drawing in the dammed.
Its walls littered with images
of
lesbians on dinner dates,
women health posters.
The doomed
are shuttled
to their shops,
offices
and
work sites.
Blood, dust,
sperm, cancer,
dirt,
flowing,
clotting
cascading stair wells,
spilling from the open wound of station exits.

Sep 22

Asset Summit

Pools of delusion,
masked by technological solutions.
Magicians
and asset managers.

Drones and rust,
artificial Intelligence.
Foundations
and
Piers.
Exploring the murky depths of future states.

Sep 22

The Hunger Hurts

The hunger hurts,
knotted stomach,
disorientation.
A triangulation of pain
stretched out in twisted
and
closed Deltas,
suffocating the blood,
etching painful tributaries along cords of tangled nerves.

Sep 22

Who kills a nine-year old?

Sep 22

Pet poochies

Jelly headed woman
and their pet poochies.
How is it that those
foul
four legged f...........
can catapult grown woman
into a monologue
of inarticulate,
senseless drivel
whilst their pathetic
wet
rubber
snouts
weld themselves
to
another poochies deathly anus?

Sep 22

Post Goth

He had been poured into his cheap white shirt.
A white rubber tire,
tree rings of Guinness and black
marked his lost years.
The wet
spongy remains of a young Goth,
crushed under the weight of the corporate machine.

Sep 22

Empiriomonism

Empririomonism,
Bogdanov was real,
the world was real,
no delusion,
no chasm
between the physiological and the psychical.
Just slate grey mornings
and tired pigeons.

Death of the Queen

'Hyperbole will be redefined'
with the death of the Queen.
England reboots,
while the evils of monarchy
are quietly filed away,
suspended,
like coat hangers in a forgotten luggage room.
Glitz and pomp
will fill the coming months.
A media carousel
of recycled jingoism.
A disinfectant
dissolving the true particles of horror
that line the pages of the 'History of the Monarchs'.

Sep 22

Frustration

Frustration
entombed within an iron sphere
suspended
by spidery webs of time
gently swinging between Zeno's termini.

Sep 22

The pepper pot women
in their polka dot dresses.

Sep 22

Sunday morning — ruined

The Sunday morning God Squad are here.
The men: Cheap suits on bikes
armed with halo caustic biblical fictions
under their arms
bound in blood and skin.
They've come to scare the children
and the old.
Overweight, pious women
in pairs
Peering through windows
sweeping for victims.
A legion of simpletons and sadists
masochists and martyrs
deployed from some filthy chasm
to spoil my morning.

Sep 22

Untitled

Lips of Scarlet,
shoes of Gold.

I'm only a crack in a castle of glass.

Sep 22

London has gone mad

London has gone mad.
A sea of people
fill Euston station concourse
spilling out into Eversholt and Melton Street.
The swarm is arrested,
held captive behind the metal trellis
of the Underground Station.
Flags,
banners,
rucksacks
suitcases.
The world has come to London.
An Elizabeth frenzy has begun!

Sep 22

Untitled

He was like a heavy, empty, wooden wardrobe.

Sep 22

Alpha

Alpha,
Ambulance,
Ash.
The first cool breeze.
A sky harder than granite.
Filaments of smoke
whirl and draw out X Ray lines
that drift across the cycle path.

Sep 22

Untitled

Angry buses
clatter over
lonely
speed bumps.

Sep 22

 zra

Limbs filled,
and
mingled,
like flesh heaped in a bin
and here an arm upward,
clutching a fragment of marble.

Sep 22

Dark Jewels

The thin liquorice leather
Nips at her neck.
Dark jewels,
Clink,
Clink,
Clink.

Sep 22

Clean

I long for something clean,
freshly cut silk,
a blade,
a broken bundle of mirrors,
Or
fractured edges of moonlight
buried in the gypsum desert.

Sep 22

Red Mist

Atomised,
Red mist.
A cloud of blood
drifting over
a shattered
Artic,
porcelain landscape.

Sep 22

Her Face

Her face
like a bleached continent.
Her mouth,
a small narrow slit,
Paper cut.
Her eyes,
small watery,
lifeless pools.
Her Diplodocus neck reaches out
of a tablecloth of black satin,
that
envelopes,
rolls of marbled flesh.
Her hair.
strands of illuminous emerald
and
cerulean
arrested by a machete

Sep 22

Collate

Collate,
collate,
collate.
Why do we accept?
Solipsism.
Sleep walking
across the trenches.
No wish to probe
rolling over is easy.
Spirals of ineptitude
made from iron coils,
sinking in the sands of time

Sep 22

Dry friable earth
Going from dust to more dust.
The great concert of the winds.

Sep 22

Crowbars

Crowbars
and
Carpets.
Black cats on car roofs.
All the mornings
Piled up along the curb stones.
Where the dead walked
and the living were made of cardboard.

Sep 22

Flame Burns

Flame burns,
rain sinks into the cracks.
Entropy spreads like an unceasing plague,
Beneath the thud of the years.

Sep22

Screeching Sentence

Every screeching sentence,
like a box of pins,
scattered across the wooden floor.
Walls soaked with teenage angst.
Tension pervades
every crevice,
crack
and
contour.

Sep 22

Basildon Crow

The jaws
of the sliding doors
at Basildon
let the cry of the Crow in.

Sep 22

Rollercoaster

Threading screams through the sky,
the Rollercoaster roars
as the cooling September Sea,
reclines.

Sep 22

Apparition of the coming Winter

Indian jewels.
Apparition of the coming Winter,
drawn out by a slab of sky.
Restless shadows,
dance and die,
eclipsed,
severed by a tired day.

Sep 22

The Queen is buried today

I want to disturb the
pretence,
pomp,
sever the enforced mourning,
I mow the grass.
In the trees and sky
the Parrots, Black Birds, Crows, Magpies
chatter and swirl
on the perimeter of
the targeted hysteria.

Sep 22

Thales

Phusis,
Kosmos,
Physics.
Origin and growth.
Thales mind flows,
droplets gather,
surface tension builds,
pools of existence form.

Sep 22

Dentist

Tension was rising
as the grey wash of the sky descended.
The drunks behind the bus station were catatonic,
yelping,
howling.
Electricity crackled
in the waxy evening.
The littered pavements
had been slain,
exhausted and stretched out,
dividing the filthy grass.
Steel frames
being dismantled
clanging,
collapsing
into the back of grimy vans.
The last of the cheap market goods
bundled into the dark

Sep 22

Claires mum

Claires mums in trouble,
fell out of her bed
at seventy-three.
Swollen throat from surviving cancer.
All is quiet
now the sun has set on Whips Cross Hospital.

Sep 22

Pre-Socratics

Buoyant Thales in his liquid universe.
Anaximander's symmetrical,
unchanging,
motionless
world.
Anaximenes breathed and lived air!
Pythagoras embraced the soul,
forever, life!
Alcmaeon sensed existence in the mirror.
Xenophanes, a sceptic,
knew the limits of minds and gods.
Heraclitus unified the opposites in a universe of continual
flux.

Sep 22

Overcast Sky

In an overcast sky
the roaming star
vibrates and jostles.
A pizza cutter disk,
steely wheeled,
slices through
an atmosphere of tar.

Last Days of Summer

Pillars form in the sky
In the last days of summer.
Crows fight on the roof tops
as my brain percolates in tired associations and thoughts.
Trees animated by
blustery breezes,
bend and dance.
Each green leaf will soon turn,
dying sunlight
and
senescence.

Mini Budget

Let the bankers write their own cheques!
Restart the cycle of financial collapse,
Wind up the money train.
arms deals,
narcotics,
government investments,
offshore accounts
billionaires.
Top tier saturation in the green stuff.
Meanwhile,
food banks multiply in the rubble of democracy.
The real workers are voiceless,
hungry,
their vision dissembled,
brick by brick.
Right winged middle-class parasites
roll along like t in a pipe
with the idolatry for the rich,
themselves only a couple of stops,
or a few grand,
from the queue at the foodbank.

The old will shiver.
Baby boomers sigh at a broken Europe
that their parents defended,
died for.
Now too poor to switch on the heating,

they are scolded by the words of the elite,
financial clowns,
elected by no one
to spend freely from the public purse
without regulation
or
law.
The value of our old people,
the value of modern history
is like coal,
few respect the time taken for it to form,
many profit from its instant warmth.

Volleyball AGM

Skeletons and clocks,
scarlet red coils,
bifurcating fibres,
schematically draw out the nervous system.
Entwined,
twisted.
Measuring tape in a double helix,
bones and cells
ground into paste.
A poster of deconstructed life for the kids.

Sep 22

Thales Dies

Thales dies.
To die of heat and thirst
whilst being a spectator at a gymnast contest.
It was his time,
he could no longer see the stars from the Earth.

Sep 22

Magma Oceans

Magma oceans
cooling to form the Earth's crust.
Fossilised beaches,
aprons of sand,
layered strata units.
Ancient landscapes frozen in time.

Sep 22

Untitled

Scarlet red scrolls
litter the seabed
with human industry.

Sep 22

Jannis Kounellis

Jannis Kounellis
came back to me today
in a sack,
full of carbon and diamonds

Sep 22

Cosmos

Carrying echoes of its own youth,
the cosmos' signature
glitters with photons,
scattered across fourteen billion years.
Dance across the cosmos

Sep 22

Beaches

Beaches,
devoid of everything but quartz.
Multi storey buildings,
skeletal structures in sand.
Chemical gardens
stretch out in terrestrial planes under the microscope.

Bonds
breaking down into hydrocarbons,
leaking life.
Charged ions
rendering salty seas.
Carbonate ions,
coupled,
linked,
chains,
towers of life.

Villains of industry
incarcerated in limestone cells,
sleeping in ridges where light cannot penetrate

Sep 22

Neolithic Children

Neolithic Children
hidden in the chamber of souls,
wait for the pencil of first light
to break the black iron dawn.

Sep 22

Untitled

Wet, glossy pools
sometimes smooth
other times scarred.

Sep 22

Untitled

Atomised cadmium yellow
contained under the crushing force of
acrid slabs of phthalo green

Sep 22

Iron Belly

Iron belly
canon,
glowing.
Distant tunes descend.
Under me,
time and space curve.

Sep 22

Marylebone Station

All the people shuffling up the platform
to the ticket barriers,
past the rows of bikes,
a ramshackle of frames and handlebars,
lonely and defeated.
An early morning mist,
suspended from the road bridge consumes the end of the
platform,
penetrated only by a sea of red lights,
Illuminating the edge of the sharp gantry.

Fog peppered by slices of red LEDs,
fragmented,
diced lights.

Sep 22

Metropolitan Line

Racks and racks
of cables, clinging to rhythmic grids.
Geometry of information,
signals.
A billion crucifixions
stapled to miles of fences.
Hung and clipped
from iron hooks
by plastic cable ties.
Intersecting with junction boxes,
a woven, multi coloured fabric
containing highways of electrons.
Sprawling along the backs of gardens,
gently undulating,
escaping over elegant arches.

Oct 22

Untitled

On my knees at 5 am,
Italy slides by,
the room shivers.

Oct 22

Untitled

Two towers.
Two planes.
To wake in terror!

Compression,
locked in,
Stiff.
Wasted hours
pile up under the windows, obscuring the horizon.

Oct 22

Blake

I see the Past, Present and Future,
existing all at once before me.

Oct 22

Untitled

Future states, determined points,
determined points, future states.
A little resonance here, a little resonance there.
Probable future states multiply.

Oct 22

Untitled

Rotational symmetry,
translational symmetry
symmetry breaking.
Lipstick on the rim of a wine glass

Quantum systems can be in many states at once,
a phenomenon known as 'superposition'.
Observe a quantum system – take a measurement – system
collapses.

Oct 22

Symmetries

Rotational symmetry,
broken,
lipstick on a wine glass.
Translational symmetry,
broken,
a broken panel in a fence.

Watch the wave function collapse.
The precarious superposition
unfolds before its realised.
What hides behind the curtain?

Oct 22

Morbidly Obese Women

Morbidly obese women
waddle down the aisles,
gasping from breath,
pausing at every head rest.
Steadying their mass against the lateral force of the moving
train.

Oct 22

Discovering the Big Bang

How cruel,
Le Maitre, the Belgian Priest fathered the Big Bang!
Was it an accident that it aligned so well to a creation story?

Oct 22

Ceramic Skin

Ceramic skin,
dark,
soft,
short,
hair
against my cheek.

Black spider,
washing machine drum

Oct 22

Station Hotel

Muffled Gregorian chants.
Grey worn out pin stripe suit.
Why does he make everything so difficult?
Swaying like a broken fence in a pretence of fragility.

Oct 22

Slope Stability

Pinball Hydrology,
Pluvial,
Fluvial,
Snow melt and silver spheres,
fired and cracked under glass.

Hydrostatic rebound,
tens of thousands of years of movement.
Liquid bricks,
slope angle,
broken watches.

Oct 22

We are all wired

We are all wired,
scattered across the dusty terrain,
passionate and determined to change the world forever.

Broken engineers stitched together – common consequence.

Oct 22

Conkers

My dad brought out a bag of conkers
pre-strung and ready for blitzing!
In the right position
the low October sun,
kept us warm
as the conkers cracked against the fence
and their soft white bellies
lay strewn across the grass.

Oct 22

Heroic Moths

Heroic Moths were drawn to the sodium lights.
Then the night came,
and the lights went out
as the cities burned.

Oct 22

Dans Sunflowers

Sunflowers dumbly stare South
satellite dishes,
desperate and parasitic,
their cheap wings,
open sails
feeding off the streams of photons.

Oct 22

'Caution The Blast!'

'CAUTION THE BLAST!'
says the sign at the runway.
There's only about ten people on this
toothpaste tube of a plane,
accelerating down the runway,
on a pair of cheap roller skates,
past Pagodas and Tugs,
lifeless tombs in medieval ponds.

I hate golf courses
and blue pens.

Oct 22

New Haircut

New haircuts
and
robotic poetry.
Teachers that exorcise all creativity from the flow of young
neurons.
Come home to the music,
far from the school yards of hell

Oct 22

Stuck on the North Circular Road

Time hangs off the car bumper in front of me.
Car pressed against car,
in the stone cold dak of night.
Traffic welded to the North Circular Road
in cold fusion.
Lights flicker in the hospital,
as they weight of the day is crushed into the fearless tarmac.

Oct 22

School

Split lip,
winded in the changing room
by a blow to the chest.
On my knees,
unable to catch my breath.

Oct 22

Hawk

The hawk fell,
folded in the grass
collapsed upon its prey,
ending the afternoon.
Shafts of dwindling light
crack open evenings curtain,
the backdrop to a gentle drama.

Oct 22

1540 AD

Five hundred years
stare back at me in this room.
Empty chairs beg for company,
the walls ache with the compression of time.
Shadows dance in the fireplace,
stepping in and out of existences

Oct 22

G. K. Chesterton

Signal boxes,
Houses of life and death.
Post boxes,
sanctuaries of human words.

Oct 22

Placoderms

Bad tempered Placoderms
swimming around in my head.
Silurian nightmares,
Devonian daydreams.

Oct 22

Comet 21P/Giacobini Zinnar

A brief encounter
with a Draconid meteor
in a back garden in Suffolk,
etched a toothpick of light
onto the heavy fabric of the Suffolk night.

Oct 22

Late Afternoon Sun

Late afternoon sun,
Illuminates the zig zag catenary,
the crossover,
the platform end.
Electricity and steel,
thread themselves into the distance,
stretching west, touching the dying embers of another day.

Chips and fags,
kids dressed in white Karate Whites

Cardboard Men

Like over erect penises,
the cardboard men,
in their corrugated suits
cruise the corridors of the third floor.
Over excited schoolboys
pretending to be men,
hover anxiously outside meeting room doors,
desperate to pour
toxic rumours into each other's ears,
fuelling in humane,
silent executions for the older guard,
who are taken by surprise,
caught sleeping.

Oct 22

Bathroom Landscape

Horizontal meets plain.
White sealant forms a gypsum beach
halted by a sea of stone.
Shadows intersect the cliff,
bleached light
punctured by a dark echo.

Charity is the power of defending that which we know to
be indefensible.
Charity to the deserving is not charity at all,
but justice.

Oct 22

Parents Evening

Her eyes were like
two dead insects,
sitting behind a cage of wire and glass.
Greasy, limp strands of hair
fell off her shoulder.
Her forehead was like damaged plaster board,
expressionless,
closed.
She filled the classroom with her sterility.

Oct 22

Crepuscular Rays

Crepuscular rays
form a pyramid in the sky,
its base cemented in the granite green slab of sea.

Oct 22

October Sky

The sky opens up
like a wet sack of offal,
bearing its continuous grey innards,
peeled back,
enveloping the entire sky.

Oct 22

Giant white Craniums

Giant, white craniums
trampling up and down the street
with boxes.
Bent skulls at the bus stop.

Oct 22

Red Wine

Pain, scattered across the waste land.
Red wine bleeds in wet soil.
A black and white cat
surveys the silent morning
from the top of a wheelie bin.
The streets are empty,
time suspended,
hanging from the telephone wires.

Oct 22

Storm

A razor blade of time
flashed in and out of existence
under the weight of the thunderstorm.

Oct 22

Copper Mill

Coils of razor wire,
sharply define the perimeter of the reservoir,
forming empty cylinders,
that frame the wet sky.
Interrupted by power lines in the middle distance,
the steel monoliths,
exchange information.

Oct 22

Waiting for Ben

A car park full of murderers.
Plastic devices,
flap around in the wind,
like old men's testicles.
Polythene sacks,
with cut throats
hang from fence posts.
I share the peace of this place with a Raven.

Oct 22

Francis Bacon

Bacon died freezing a chicken
and magic made metaphysics.
A ships navigation determined by magic or mechanics.
Sails and compass,
Physics and Metaphysics.
Elementary forms,
obscure characters,
hidden material,
individually make up the whole.
In the head,
judgement or appetite?
Recognition of fetishes,
bias,
diversions from the pursuit of truth.
Discipline,
research.

Bacons Idols
1. The Tribe
2. The Den
3. The Market Place
4. The Theatre

Oct 22

Paper Thin Thoughts

My thoughts,
paper thin,
kicked up like leaves
in a gentle whirlwind,
failing to settle.

Oct 22

DLR

A rollercoaster ride in the evening peak.
The hunting if the wheels,
ski slope gradients,
a marvel of engineering.
A robotic future for public transport.

Oct 22

Canal

With their big white faces
and their black, bat like capes
flapping behind them in a violent vortex,
the two wheeled phantoms emerge from the dusk,
temporarily marking a fleeting existence
through tyre tracks
in the drying pavement.

Oct 22

Sky over Southend – on – Sea

Plastic bins,
scattered in warfare by armies of bin men.
Blaspheme and light aircraft
fill the sky over Southend – On – Sea.

A seven- foot Python
swallowed
a fifty four-year old woman.

Oct 22

Kant

Kant's contrasting arguments
amount to contradictory conclusions.
Hegel's dialectic.
From the union of 'Being and Unbeing'
Comes
'Becoming'.

Oct 22

Pumpkins and Pianos

Pumpkins and Pianos
A filthy brick
floats on a Sea of wood,
navigated by a lazy mop.
Tin foil tortured by a perpetual breeze.
Pressure transitions,
etched onto the surface.
The mapping of shiny scars.

Oct 22

The Man with small arms

The man with small arms
is dreaming of the cattle market.
A thousand litres of warm blood
trickle over the cobblestones
and
pool under the witches' ball.

Rectangular Hell

Rectangular hell,
connected by a labyrinth of alley ways,
curbs and slopes,
in lost syncopation.
Walls and fences slide past
like a giant organic puzzle.
Black street – lamps
loom on corners.
Tarmac repairs
litter cul-de-sacs,
everything is out of key.

Oct 22

The Field

The whooping Kites
circle above the field,
dive behind the hedgerow.
Striations of dark, plump earth
illuminated by emerald shoots stretch out
in undulating chicanes,
out to the dark bar.

Oct 22

Poles, Posts and Pipes

Poles, posts, pipes and chimney stacks
lose their dimensions,
gain their definition
as they morph into silhouettes.
The detail of the day,
swept aside,
as the light fades,
but there is no one on the call.
Perhaps a silent apocalypse has occurred?
No sign of existence.

Nov 22

All the useless Doctors

All the useless Doctors,
that should have retired,
or
should have been struck off.
Every day,
murdering the old and infirm
whilst medical care
is deployed from the back of ambulances.
Waiting for the next vacant bed,
eating lunches from plastic trays
in
sterile
corridors.

Nov 22

Marble Halls

Marble Halls
eat my brain.
Carpets of terror
rolled across polished wooden floors.
The stink of aristocracy,
decay,
mental illness,
brain damage from consuming their own faeces.

Nov 22

Nurse said

Nurse said
her blood pressure
is OK for now.
They are checking it
4 hourly.
Doctor will see her
at 9AM tomorrow,
and then they have a meeting
at 11AM.
We can call after that.

Nov 22

Young Boy – North Circular

Young boy,
captured in the web of concrete,
encircling,
him and his mother.
Framed by the motorway,
staring into the stagnant canal below.

Nov 22

Two empty chairs

Two empty chairs,
staring West.
The winds of death
seep through my slippers.
Parrots circle
an invisible gravitational well.
Anthocyanins stain the leaves,
they will drop with the first frost.

Nov 22

Spooked

I am spooked by the scuttle,
and empty time,
hanging over the hearth,
buses at termini
in isolated country villages,
silent erect telegraph poles,
kept at sail by woven steel cables,
buried deep along the hedgerow
with the rotting earth
and the clays,
arresting all animation,
whilst billowing clouds transit
the dead,
open space.

Nov 22

Firework Display

Flames licked the edges
of the
cold,
black,
tar of night,
underneath the Lion tamers pole.
With a face of poison,
the overweight,
teenage fire warden
puffs out his chest
and
sucks
and
sucks
on cigarette
after
cigarette
to a colosseum
of pathetic
parents.
They are seated,
hunched,
shoulder to shoulder,
a hermetic wall of human despair.
Their children
clinging to chrome water bottles
with brand new mittens,

fixated
with innocent eyes
at the spectacle.
From behind double glazing
in his first floor flat,
like Julius Caesar,
stands a bare-chested man,
occasionally illuminated
by the
orange glow from the flames.
In the corner
of the damp field,
the sticky darkness
is broken,
by a bar of toxic white light.
Silhouetted figures
jostle in a doorway,
eventually making their way out
onto the grass,
led by yellow dots of light
from their pocket torches.
Glowing firelighters,
stretch out and ignite
the first fireworks of the display
as tiny red embers
dance and fall
from above.

Nov 22

Telephone Wires

Telephone wires
dissect the tree.
Galaxies of stars
form on the tip of each branch.
In every drop,
a
Multiverse.

Nov 22

$\mathcal{P}$assed $\mathcal{O}$pportunities

Passed opportunities,
junctions?
or
Loops?
Bifurcations in time
and
circumstance
all leading to the same point,
the present.

Nov 22

Euston Plaza

Splinters of nuclear light
detonate off the wet pavement
from a low afternoon sun.
A train of school kids
in high viz jackets
pew out of the underground station
onto Euston Plaza.
Debris from an electronic cigarette
hung in the scattered light,
ethereal animals,
deteriorating forms.
Elf like men
hide in the shadows of the Weatherspoon's,
watching to world
slowly ground to an end.

Nov 22

Yellow Shoes

Twats wearing last year's masks,
yellow shoes,
leather trousers.
Brain washed zombies,
file up and down platforms.
Will London ever recover from the Pandemic?
Cro magnon man
with his headphones,
lady with grey leggings
pulled up so high
her extremities are an advertisement
for sanitary towels.
A man with a Crow nose
in a plum-coloured hat.
Pale blue surgical masks
turn my stomach
and my mind.

Adidas
Jeans
Puffer Jacket
Ankle Socks
Nike Rucksack
Surgical Mask
Seven Sisters.

Nov 22

The Doric

He walked into the bar stool,
his eyes are bad,
awkward hands
eclipsed by slippery pint glasses,
different shapes,
different form.,
The Eagle has landed!
discharged,
executed with precision
onto the wet,
Wooden platform.

Nov 22

Sea Surface Temperatures in the Atlantic
Are high for November.
18 °C forecast in the Midlands today.
Nurses about to strike.
National Grid
announce
planned power outages.

Binary Stars

Binary stars
reflect,
run in parallel
into the cool,
evening light,
deformed by double glazing.
Photosynthesis,
unplugged,
bare.
Broken limbs
revealed,
undressed,
undignified.
All of nature
slumped in a corridor
waiting for an asteroid impact,
or,
a giant coronal mass ejection.

Nov 22

The digging never stops

The digging never stops,
cranes bow in shame,
twinkling orange lights blink
as tons of concrete
is poured into caverns,
suffocating the tired earth.

Nov 22

Face

Gelatinous face,
poured like wet cement into a head scarf,
featureless,
with the exception
of a pitted,
weathered surface,
enveloped by a thin material
held together by a bow.

Nov 22

Biosphere

Injected,
extracted.
The mutilated cadaver
of the biosphere,
stretched out on the morgues table.
The stench of death,
hidden for now,
lurking in every crack, crevice, wound,
every sun set,
every ocean floor, just beneath the crust.
A magma of poison
making its way slowly to the surface,
waiting to erupt,
explode.
Consume and envelope
the empty,
decaying
shell.

Nov 22

1776

Smith divided labour,
nature dissembled.
Switch on the viable machine,
inject,
extract,
mutilate her.
She does not scream,
instead,
gently falls asleep,
loses consciousness
under the weight
of the invisible poison.
Eventually,
her expired body
will slump and fall.

Nov 22

Wealth of Nations

Don't just bite the hand that feeds you.
Dissect it,
burn it,
re-burn it,
then
poison it.
Then
pretend
all along
that you cared.

Nov 22

Remembrance Sunday

In a super-hero cape,
compete with the dog collar
and
hypocrisy hanging on her lips,
the local Minister
expounds stories of God,
Jesus
with nonsense of 'dying for one's country'.
Beavers,
Squirrels,
Guides,
Cubs
and Scouts,
perched in rows,
fused to cold metal chairs.
All in uniform,
little soldiers,
learning from the past.

Nov 22

ill

Grey, blue sky fell,
splintered into a million pieces
in front of the Town Hall.
Bag pipes
and
drums.
108 million have fallen.
Falklands,
Northern Ireland.
Medals gleaming.
Teachers and Laphroaig
as the Scouts
and
Councillors
lay wreaths.

Nov 22

The Dentist Chair

In the Dentist Chair again.
Soft tissue of tongue
lacerated
by a jagged coastline of metal fillings,
exposed by masticatory erosion,
imbibing.
Decaying teeth,
clinging on to the permanence of past interventions.
Old welds,
give up under the stress,
uncouple from the piles driven deep
into
the Erath's crust of my jaw.
Another temporary filling,
forged by the Alchemist
in the corner of this
cell of pain.

Nov 22

St Pancras

Barbaric, pink, neon,
stained yellow clock face,
embroidered with gold trimming.
Sky blue girders.
A ceaseless unhappening,
clings to the brutal,
steel benches
in St Pancras Station.

Loughborough Rain

Soaked cement
exposed,
first floor,
bleeding with rain,
aching with the afternoon.
Mirrors form
in depressions
where curb meets road.
Cold ochre light
weighs heavy
on the naked trees
over Loughborough Town.

Clouds pile up
in the North,
A fake mountain-chain
in the
diminishing light.

Nov 22

Prussian Blue

Prussian Blue
like a jewel in the pot,
poured over Crimson and Umber.
Lake,
wall,
sky.
Iridescent prisms,
surface glitters.

Tectonic Tensions

Tectonic tensions,
two people
completely out of syncopation.
Driving a stake
slowly, through youth,
innocence,
promise,
haemorrhaged across the floor.
Mutilated conversations,
broken rivers,
dislocated intentions
mobilised by chaos,
fear and spite.

Nov 22

Whiter Teeth

'Whiter teeth in just 3 days.'
A young bride,
teeth matching dress.
The 'before' and 'after' images,
one badly lit,
tinted,
stained,
the other gleaming
under angelic light.
How stupid do they think we are?

Nov 22

Teeth & Yates

Teeth fall apart,
the centre cannot hold,
Mere anarchy is loosed upon the world.

Nov 22

Milankovitch Futures

Spatula of ice,
Milankovitch futures,
ice ages,
piled upon,
ice ages.
Compression,
breath,
compression.
Distant futures – entombed until the sun retires.

Fear of the Curve

Fear of the curve
and what is beyond the protecting signal.
A menacing tunnel mouth,
a painted well,
Oily,
Inky,
Phthalo Blue.
The white eye of the cow,
a dissected hill,
thousands of years,
percolate,
bleeds through the stone.
Slivery mats
cling to the brick work
suspended in crystalline Lakes,
intersected,
divided
by sap green veins,
sodden and terrified,
silently screaming
in the bitumen lamp black.

Nov 22

Anthropocene

Anthropocene,
Red in tooth and claw.
The petulant child of rationality
is believed to exist
somewhere on an isolated island
in the Pacific Ocean.
Everywhere else
there is multiplying madness,
swollen
from gorging on toxins,
walking eye deep in hell,
we have finally synthesised with nature.

Nov 22

A & E

Broken people
wait on
broken chairs
in the hope of being fixed
they come here,
but are often turned away.
Night rattles,
in the corners of the room
as each hour
drags its heavy body by.

Nov 22

Ice Ages

Ice ages
Stacked in my DNA.
Bones frozen
in the tundra of my being.
A permafrost has set in,
under my skin,
penetrating my internal organs.

Nov 22

Untitled

Reservoirs of hate
hide in the mountains.

Nov 22

A thousand Suns

A thousand suns
Isotope bingo,
an enrichment of Carbon 14.
Radioactive babies,
half a century lost,
Scattered in the mushroom clouds of atomic testing.

Nov 22

Interglacial

A punctuated,
brief,
comfortable
existence
in each interglacial.
Separated by 100,000 years of paralysis.
Nature entombed,
cryogenically suspended.

Nov 22

Ashen

Ashen,
broken,
uncoupled plasticity of skin.
Face like Grantham,
with a 12th century landscape in her eyes,
incongruity through a touch screen.

Nov 22

Juggernaut

Mass, force,
juggernaut of protons
colliding with the meridian,
a spray of particles
across the dual carriage way.
Subatomic array,
building up on
wind screens
and
dashboards.
Slow unravelling of elements over the asphalt.

Nov 22

Saturday morning — Birmingham

Two eyes
Two bullet holes
Double barrel shotgun of photons
penetrates the bedroom
on an early Saturday morning.
The suburbs of Birmingham
are stirring
under the hard edge of this
cold atomic light.
Grey towers
lean into a slab of sky.
A vail of Naples Yellow
hangs over the horizon,
pinned by cranes and spires.

Nov 22

Wonder

Have I strayed too far from wonder?
Does everything need to be hard edges,
contrasts
and razor-sharp intersections?
Harmonic,
jostle,
bleed,
resonate in sympathy with one another.
A vast swell of symphonies,
sweeps in
spoiling voids,
the ringing of parallel worlds.

Humility

Humility sits like a broken vase on a corner table.
Queues get longer for the food bank.
China will lead the way
to a six degrees warmer world,
where,
vitreous oceans
harbour calcareous forms
no more.
The crowbar of inept politics
wielded high.
Victims choose
whether to eat or be warm.
Suffocating madness
born from a lack of vision,
a lack of intent.
A calving of human dreams
and
innovation.
Sleep walking through the sixth extinction.

Nov 22

Leigh

Thames Estuary retreated,
miles of jewel studied mud exposed
to radiant pins of November light.
Southend University Hospital
stares out to Kent
while the silvery water
threads its way
through the harbour,
a mercurial intestine.

Nov 22

St Pauls

St Pauls stands proud,
its dome penetrating
a heavy wave of early morning fog.
White latticed spokes
and
taught woven cables
hold up the great wheel,
plugged into the bank of the river Thames.
Tired faces
file over the bridge
to the background clattering
of
metal on metal.
Vaporous trains
dissolve into Charing Cross Station.

Nov 22

Days locked in stasis,

silent wires divide the sky,
Crows flap between the trees.

Nov 22

Tourists and Terrorists

As the city burns
tourists and terrorists
shuffle in and out of
shops and museums.
The city skyline
aches under the weight
of a million souls.

Dec 22

North Circular Road

Badly drawn
telegraph towers
etched onto a pink sky
mark my transit,
as I drive
on the elevated section of the North Circular,
heavy cast,
heading East,
on an early winter morning.
I have suffered the atrocity of sunrises.

Dec 22

A beautiful blade of Italy,
pouring sweet harmonics
across the air-conditioned room.
A thousand generations
of sculpted genetics,
cured,
perfected
by the centuries.

Dec 22

Astronomy Night

Mars; perfect visibility.
Jupiter; until Saturday 0106.
Saturn; until Friday 2124.
Uranus; until Saturday 0536.
Neptune; until Saturday 0031.

Dec 22

Jupiter

Jupiter
pinned behind dust,
out of focus.
White crescent.
Yellow orb.
White domes.
Pocked,
pocked.
Layers of catastrophe
pooled on the retina.

Dec 22

Choked Oceans

Choked oceans,
subduction ceases.
The torn belly of Earth,
exposed
and
acidified.
Cold,
murky depths
stagnate.
Methane Hydrate,
blisters the edges of the sky,
Filters into the depths,
cancerous,
caverns
form.
Interior fear.
The bowels,
shocked,
Annealed fractures,
unfolding stasis.
The inaction of lungs,
terminated igneous.
Drying out like a dead pheasant
from an unnamed spiral arm
in a distant galaxy.

Dec 22

Fungi

Mycorrhizal,
neural,
networks of Fungi
flourish on the forest floor.
In the wake of the storm.
Radiation of carpets
across
wet,
decomposing
oceans of Earth.
Soft wet cushions,
punctuate sodden tree bark
Cling to each other
like commuters,
side by side,
waiting for a train
under the canopy of a fallen Oak.
Ephemeral,
ectoplasmic forms
welded to Birch,
float like searching souls
through the thick fog of transpiration
and
broken rays of dying photons.

Dec 22

Ivory Horses

Ivory Horses
radiate electric light
with the warm glow of grandparents.
Museum of the dead.
Frames full of fading faces,
Christmas and New Year,
a yearning for their distant voices
to break the distance of years,
Decades and half centuries.
Beetroot and Butter.
Fans coil
inside plastic coal.
They all sat there once,
pipe smoke,
the crackle of vinyl,
movement now ceased.
Thoughts and sounds hang
recorded in the woven fabric of each armchair.
Contrasts and patterns
clashing and banging,
nothing smooth,
all tilted and 'off set'.
Readers Digest
rattle and lean
controlled by dark mahogany.

Blistered oil paint,
lay dead in white plastic frames,
uncomfortable, ill at ease,
desperately hanging on until the end.

Dec 22

Clay shrinks

Clay shrinks,
Crow's feet.

Smoker's lips.

Desiccation,
Deformation.

Recumbent folds
Collapsed toes.

Geometry of space and time
out of gauge.

Fractured joints,
dislocation.

Signals flicker
out of correspondence.

Dec 22

A pale elegance

A pale elegance
drawn across her face,
humility filled her eyes.

From her plain features
a caring, intellectual kindness radiated,
as the low sun illuminated Twyford Railway Station.

Dec 22

Frost

Like a coat of emulsion
a frost has descended upon us
encasing everything in a brittle frame.

The morning is silent and still,
paralysed and entombed
in the icy crust.

An orange beam,
softens the hard edges,
a low morning Sun

Brings relief
to the other worldly feel
of a Jupiter moon.

ABOUT THE AUTHOR

 Brian Douglas Haddock lives and works in London. He has a PhD in Fine Art from Reading University and is a visiting Professor at Newcastle University and Loughborough University.

Lightning Source UK Ltd.
Milton Keynes UK
UKHW010752161222
414025UK00001B/20

9 781728 379524